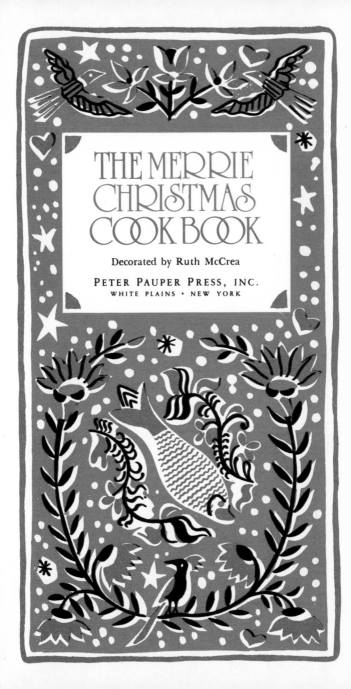

THE MERRIE CHRISTMAS COOK BOOK

Decorated by Ruth McCrea

PETER PAUPER PRESS, INC.
WHITE PLAINS · NEW YORK

CHRISTMAS DAY

The stockings deck the chimney,
The goose is hanging high,
And Mother's in the kitchen
Baking Christmas pie!

Sister pins the mistletoe,
Hoping to be kissed,
Mother bastes the turkey,
And trusts she won't be missed!

Brother trims the Christmas tree,
Loops the boughs with snow,
While Mother, busy Mother,
Is always on the go.

Father's in the pantry,
Sampling Yuletide rum,
Full of inner happiness,
Can't you hear him hum?

Come, leave the kitchen, Mother,
We want to drink a toast!
Here's a merry Merry Christmas
To the one we love the most!

HOLIDAY CANAPÉS

Holiday Canapés

AMERICAN CHEESE AND BACON

Cut American cheese to fit triangles of bread which have been toasted on one side. Place cheese on untoasted side, and top with a bit of sliced bacon. Broil until bacon is crisp.

ANCHOVY PUFFS

Mix ½ cup butter and one 3-ounce package cream cheese; add 1 cup flour. Chill. Roll very thin and cut with 2-inch cookie cutter. Spread with anchovy paste; fold over; bake in 400° oven 10 minutes. Serve hot.

ANCHOVY SPREAD

Mix equal parts of chopped anchovies, mashed Roquefort cheese and butter. Blend together until smooth and serve on Melba toast.

CRAB AU GRATIN

1 can crabmeat
½ cup sharp Cheddar cheese, grated
Sherry

Toast one side of a slice of white bread, butter the untoasted side, and spread with crabmeat. Sprinkle crabmeat thickly with grated cheese, and broil until cheese is melted. A moment before removing from broiler, pour on a tablespoon of sherry, heat and cut into triangles.

CRABMEAT AND SOUR CREAM DIP

2 cups crabmeat, shrimp or lobster
1½ cups sour cream
Salt and pepper
Sweet pickle relish

Combine seafood with sour cream, add relish, season to taste. Sprinkle with chopped parsley or paprika. Serve with potato chips or crackers, as a dip.

CHICKEN LIVER PATÉ

3 chicken livers
3 eggs, hard-boiled
1 onion, minced
Salt and pepper

Cook chicken livers until tender. Fry onions until golden brown. Combine all ingredients in wooden bowl, seasoning with salt and pepper to taste. Chop until fine, and serve on crackers or toast.

CREAM CHEESE PUFFS

2 packages cream cheese
1 egg
½ teaspoon onion, grated

Beat cream cheese with egg until thoroughly blended, light and smooth. Add grated onion, and heap on rounds of bread, toasted on one side. Broil about 1 minute, or until brown and puffy. Serve hot.

CHEESE BISCUITS

1 package snappy cheese
1/4 cup butter
1/2 cup flour
Salt

Mix well and set in refrigerator till hard. Roll to thickness of pie crust, and cut into small circles with a cordial glass. Sprinkle with paprika and bake in a 350° oven 15 minutes. Serve hot. Dough may be prepared the night before for last-minute leisure.

CURRIED SHRIMP ON TOAST

Simmer 1 cup of shrimp, cut small, in melted butter to which 1 teaspoon of curry powder has been added. Heap on hot buttered toast and serve with a dab of chutney on top of each canapé.

EGGPLANT TID-BITS

Peel eggplant, cut into cubes, dip in beaten egg and bread crumbs and fry in deep fat until golden brown. Drain on brown paper and serve.

EGGS, DEVILED WITH BACON

To the mashed yolks, add double the amount of crisply fried, crushed bacon. Moisten with catsup, a little mustard, and a little mayonnaise. Heap into halves of egg-whites.

Green is the holly,
And red is the berry;
Bring on the fixin's,
We'll feast and be merry!

MOCK CAVIAR

1 medium eggplant
2 green peppers
1 Bermuda onion
3 eggs, hard-boiled
1 sour apple
1 slice pumpernickel bread
Black olives
Salad oil
Salt and pepper

Cut eggplant into slices and bake until tender in buttered casserole. Remove peel, and add to other ingredients in a wooden chopping bowl. Chop until fine and shape into a mound.

9

CLAM PUFFS

2 packages cream cheese
1 can minced clams, well-drained
1 tablespoon sherry
Tabasco sauce

Blend ingredients and pile on rounds of bread. Broil till brown and puffy. Serve piping hot. These may also be covered with pieces of uncooked bacon, and broiled until bacon is crisp.

HOT MUSHROOMS AND ONIONS

1 pound mushrooms
2 onions, minced
Butter

Wash, but do not stem, fresh mushrooms. Slice. Mince onions. Sauté onions in butter until golden brown. Add mushrooms and cook lightly. Pile on crackers and serve hot.

HOT SARDINE CANAPÉS

1 can sardines, mashed
2 teaspoons mustard
1 tablespoon chili sauce
2 tablespoons catsup
Toast, cut into fancy shapes

Blend all ingredients, and spread on toast. Broil lightly. Or wrap a teaspoon of the sardine mixture in a slice of bacon, roll, fasten with a toothpick and bake in 350° oven until bacon is crisp.

HORSERADISH AND SHRIMP

½ pound shrimp, cooked
1 tablespoon mayonnaise
1 teaspoon horseradish
½ teaspoon lemon juice
1 tablespoon cream
Dash of mustard

Chop shrimp which have been cleaned, cooked and shelled, and mix with other ingredients. Season to taste and spread on crackers.

PATÉ DE FOIE GRAS

1 can (4½ oz.) liver paté
1 can (2 oz.) mushrooms, chopped
4 ounces butter, melted
2 tablespoons brandy

Sauté mushrooms in a little butter until slightly brown. Do not dry out. Blend mushrooms, liver and butter, and then add brandy. Chill in refrigerator overnight. Butter will rise to the top of the crock and form a thin covering.

ROQUEFORT DIP

2 packages cream cheese
Roquefort cheese to taste
1 tablespoon heavy cream
¼ teaspoon onion juice
1 tablespoon sherry

Blend all ingredients, using enough Roquefort to make a creamy consistency. Let stand a few hours, and serve with potato chips or crackers.

A glistening white Christmas
With snow on the trees,
Makes appetites hearty
And easy to please!

SARDINE AND CREAM CHEESE

1 package cream cheese
1 small can sardines, mashed
1 teaspoon onion, scraped
1 tablespoon catsup
Few drops Worcestershire sauce, lemon juice

Blend cheese and sardines, add onions, lemon juice, catsup and Worcestershire sauce. Serve chilled, on crackers.

SALAMI AND ROQUEFORT

Spread thinly sliced soft salami with mixture of Roquefort cheese, cream and grated onion. Roll into cornucopias, and fasten with toothpicks.

PICKLED BEETS

Using 1 can of whole small beets, make sauce as follows:

1 cup tarragon vinegar
2 heaping tablespoons brown sugar
1 large onion, minced
1 clove garlic, minced
1 teaspoon dry mustard
Pepper and salt

Stir mixture well and add canned whole small beets which have been heated in their own juice and juice discarded. Stir frequently. The same can be done with lima beans which have first been soaked overnight, brought to a boil and cooked gently for about 20 minutes. For lima beans, add a little minced dill and chopped parsley to the sauce.

WATERCRESS CORNUCOPIAS

Remove crusts from thinly sliced white bread, butter generously with sweet butter, and roll into cornucopias, fastening with a toothpick. Place a sprig of watercress in each cornucopia so that leafy part shows.

WESTERN SPECIAL

Spread raw ground beef which has been seasoned and mixed with a little grated onion on rounds of rye-bread. Garnish with dill pickle and mustard.

SWISS CHEESE AND CLAMS

½ cup mayonnaise
½ cup milk
¾ cup grated Swiss cheese
¾ can minced clams (well drained)
Tabasco
Onion salt

Mix mayonnaise and milk. Warm slowly over a low flame and add the rest of the ingredients. Serve as dip with crackers or potato chips.

CHEESE CUBES

3 slices fresh white bread
2 tablespoons melted butter
1 egg, well-beaten
1 cup finely grated American cheese

Cut bread in 1-inch cubes. Add butter to egg; dip bread cubes into this mixture, then roll in cheese. Bake on cookie sheet in moderate oven (350°) until cheese melts and cubes are brown. These are delicious when served with lemon-and-rum drinks.

CHUTNEY AND BACON

8 strips bacon
2 tablespoons chutney

Fry bacon until crisp, chop and mix with the chutney which has been mashed with a fork. Spread on toast rounds. Makes 1 dozen. Peanut butter may be added to the mixture, if desired.

EGG-CUCUMBER-BACON

2 hard-boiled eggs
1 cucumber
1/4 pound bacon
Mayonnaise
Ritz crackers (or substitute)

Cut bacon into 2-inch pieces and fry to crispy brown. Slice hard-boiled eggs (to shape of crackers). Wash cucumber and cut slices 1/4-inch thick, same shape as eggs and crackers. Place a slice of cucumber on cracker. Place a slice of egg on cucumber and a piece of crispy bacon on top of the egg. Top with a dot of mayonnaise, and sprinkle with chopped parsley, if desired.

CHOPPED HERRING

1 matjes herring
1 onion
3 small apples
2 hard-boiled eggs
3 slices white bread
1 tablespoon sugar
2 cooked beets (optional)

Remove crusts of bread, soak in water and squeeze dry. Put all ingredients through grinder twice and add sugar.

Note: The herring is improved by soaking in cold water for a few hours or overnight before using, to remove excess salt. Chopped herring may be sprinkled with mashed yolks of hard-boiled eggs for additional color.

Festive Entrées

ROAST TURKEY

Dress and clean turkey. Rub inside with salt and pepper. Stuff neck cavity, spreading over entire breast. Fasten opening with metal pins. Fill body cavity loosely with stuffing. Rub with butter or make paste of ½ cup butter, ¾ cup flour; spread over all parts of turkey. Place turkey breast side up in open roasting pan. Drip pan from broiler may be used if large roaster is not available. Roast uncovered in slow oven (300° to 325°) 15 to 20 minutes per pound. Turkey may be placed breast side down for first half of roasting time to allow juice to run down into breast. Baste at 30-minute intervals with mixture of melted butter and hot water. When breast and legs become light brown, cover with brown paper.

BREAD STUFFING

4 cups dry bread crumbs
1 medium-sized chopped onion, if desired
1 teaspoon salt
¼ teaspoon pepper
Sage to taste
Chopped parsley
¼ teaspoon poultry seasoning, if desired
⅓ cup melted butter
Hot water or stock to moisten

Combine bread, onion, and seasoning; add butter and sufficient liquid to moisten. Mix gently.

Allow 1 cup stuffing for each pound of poultry or game.

Celery Stuffing: Add 1 cup finely cut celery.

Chestnut Stuffing: Add 1 cup chopped celery and 3 cups boiled chestnuts, forced through ricer; use milk for liquid.

Raisin Stuffing: Add 1 cup seedless raisins, cut into pieces, and 1 cup broken walnuts, if desired.

ROAST GOOSE

Singe, remove pin feathers, then wash goose in cold water and wipe dry. Season to taste. Stuff with bread stuffing. Place breast side up on rack in roasting pan. Pour 2 cups boiling water over and cover. Roast 25 to 30 minutes per pound in moderately slow oven (325° to 350°), basting with fat every 15 minutes. Pour off fat if too much accumulates. When goose is done, garnish with cranberries and watercress, and serve with apple sauce. Gravy may be made from drippings in the pan, flour, and stock.

PRUNE STUFFING

For a 14-pound goose, prepare 10 cups fine bread crumbs made from stale bread. Mix with ¾ cup chopped onion, 2½ cups peeled, cored and coarsely chopped tart apples, 2¼ teaspoons salt, 2 teaspoons poultry seasoning and ¾-pound tenderized prunes, pitted and cut into small pieces. Moisten with 6 tablespoons melted butter and mix well.

CHICKEN AND NOODLES CACCIATORE

Select a fine 5-pound fowl, place on rack in large kettle; add 3 cups water, 2 stalks celery, 1 slice onion, and 1 teaspoon salt. Cover tightly and steam 3 to 4 hours until tender. Cool and remove meat in large pieces, reserving broth.

Cacciatore Sauce

2 tablespoons olive oil
¼ cup onions, chopped
1 clove garlic, minced
Tomatoes, No. 2½ can
12 stuffed olives
4-ounce can mushrooms, sliced
½ cup green pepper, cut in strips
1 teaspoon salt
Dash pepper
¼ teaspoon basil

Combine olive oil, onions and garlic in heavy skillet, cook over low heat gently until soft and golden. Add tomatoes, olives, mushrooms, green pepper, salt, pepper and basil. Continue cooking over low heat about 20 minutes.

Skim fat from chicken broth; measure broth and add water to make 5 cups; pour into large saucepan. Bring to a boil; add 1 tablespoon salt and 1 pound package of broad noodles. Bring to a boil again; cook 15 to 20 minutes till tender. Drain, place in shallow 2-quart casserole. Arrange chicken on noodles; pour over the sauce. Bake in 350° oven for 20 minutes. Serves 8.

Grim Melancholy, go thy way;
The goose hangs high on Christmas Day!

ARROZ CON POLLO

1 chicken (3-4 lbs.) cut in serving-size pieces
1/4 cup olive oil
1 cup rice, uncooked
1 large onion, chopped
2 cloves garlic, minced
1 pound cut green beans
2 pounds canned tomatoes
1 3-ounce can chopped mushrooms
1 4-ounce can pimientos, diced
3 tablespoons chopped parsley
1 1/2 teaspoons salt
Dash pepper

Brown chicken on both sides in hot oil in large
frying pan; drain on absorbent paper; place in

3-quart baking dish and set aside. Sauté rice in same frying pan, stirring often, until golden-brown; add onion and garlic; sauté 10 to 15 minutes, or just until onion is tender. Drain and measure liquid from beans; add water to make 1 cup; add to rice mixture with beans. Stir in tomatoes, mushrooms and liquid, diced pimientos, parsley, salt, and pepper; bring to boiling, stirring often. Pour hot tomato mixture over chicken in baking dish. Bake, covered, in moderate oven (350°) approximately 1 hour, or until rice and chicken are tender. If needed, add a little boiling water to keep mixture moist.

CHICKEN BREAST AU GRATIN

1 can condensed cream-of-mushroom
  soup, undiluted
1 teaspoon poultry seasoning
1/4 teaspoon salt
1/2 cup milk
6 large chicken breasts, frozen
1/4 cup grated American cheese

Combine soup, poultry seasoning, salt, milk, in large skillet with cover. Mix well; bring to boil over low heat. Add frozen chicken breasts. Cover and cook over low heat 15 minutes. Uncover; and carefully separate chicken pieces. Place breasts, with meaty sides down, in sauce. Cook, covered, 20 to 25 minutes longer, or until tender. In a casserole, reheat chicken in sauce, turning pieces meaty sides up. Sprinkle with cheese; put under broiler long enough to melt and brown cheese a bit. Makes 6 servings.

CHICKEN BREAST IN RED WINE

1/4 cup butter
6 large chicken breasts
1 onion, sliced
1 clove garlic, minced
2 tablespoons flour
1/2 teaspoon salt
1/4 teaspoon pepper
1 chicken-bouillon cube
1 cup hot water
12 small potatoes
1/3 cup red wine

Sauté chicken breasts in hot butter on both sides until well browned. Add onion, garlic; simmer about 10 minutes. In small bowl, combine flour, salt, pepper; slowly stir in bouillon cube dissolved in hot water; pour over browned chicken. Cook slowly, covered, about a half hour, or until chicken is tender. Add potatoes and wine; heat. Garnish with parsley. Serves 6.

BAKED PORK CHOPS

4 pork chops (1 1/2 lbs.)
1/3 cup celery, finely diced
2 Tbs. brown sugar
Juice of 1/2 lemon
1/2 tsp. salt
1/2 tsp. mustard
1/8 tsp. pepper
2 cans tomato sauce
1/2 cup water

Brown chops in vegetable shortening. Place in shallow greased baking dish. Sprinkle with celery, brown sugar, lemon juice and seasonings. Pour tomato sauce and water over chops. Cover and bake in 350° oven 1 1/4 hours. Serves 4.

MEAT BALLS STROGANOFF

1½ pounds chuck, ground
1 medium onion, grated
1 teaspoon salt
⅛ teaspoon nutmeg
⅛ teaspoon cloves
Dash pepper
1½ tablespoons fat
1½ cups water (for gravy)
1 beef-bouillon cube
3 tablespoons flour
3 tablespoons water
1 teaspoon dry mustard
1 cup sour cream
2 tablespoons chopped parsley

Combine beef, onion, salt, nutmeg, cloves, and pepper in medium-size bowl; blend lightly. Form mixture lightly into about 48 small balls. Heat fat in large frying pan with tight-fitting cover; brown meat balls on all sides; remove from pan; set aside, and pour any fat from frying pan. Place water (for gravy) and bouillon cube in same frying pan; bring to a boil. Blend flour, 3 tablespoons water, and mustard to a smooth paste in cup; gradually stir into water-bouillon mixture; blend well. Cook, stirring constantly, until gravy thickens and boils 1 minute. Place meat balls in pan; cover; simmer 5 minutes, or until meat balls are just cooked. Stir in sour cream and parsley; cook over very low heat just until piping-hot; do not boil, for gravy will curdle. Serve immediately for best culinary results.

Eat the roasted Boar with zest;
This Christmas feast is sure the best!

FLANK STEAK WITH SHERRY

2 pounds flank steak
2 teaspoons meat tenderizer
1/2 cup butter
1/2 cup sherry
Salt and pepper

Sprinkle steak with meat tenderizer and cut shallow gashes on surface in a diagonal fashion. Let stand about 20 minutes. Melt butter and mix with sherry. Brush one side of meat with the mixture and broil in hot oven 5 to 7 minutes. Turn, brush the second side and broil same length of time. Carve meat on the bias in thin slices, season, and serve with remaining basting liquid. Serves 4.

BAKED VIRGINIA HAM

Place ham fat side up on rack in open roasting pan. Do not cover. Bake in 300° oven, without water, allowing 15 to 20 minutes per pound for a large ham; 20 to 25 minutes per pound for a small ham; and 25 to 30 minutes per pound for a half ham. The shorter cooking time in each case is for tenderized hams. Roast meat thermometer registers 170° when ham is done; 160° for tenderized hams. Ham may be basted during cooking period with honey, syrup from canned fruit or cider. For the last half hour of baking, score fat in diamond shapes; stick a whole clove in each diamond and rub surface with dry mustard and brown sugar.

STUFFED CROWN ROAST OF LAMB

½ cup chopped celery
1 medium onion, chopped
2 cloves garlic, minced
3 tablespoons salad oil
4 cups soft bread crumbs or cubes
2 tablespoons chopped parsley
½ teaspoon rosemary
Salt and pepper
1 sixteen-rib crown roast of lamb
6 strips bacon
Raw potato
Flour
Currant jelly

Set oven at 325°. Sauté celery, onion and garlic in oil until almost tender. Add bread crumbs, parsley, rosemary, 1 teaspoon salt and pepper to taste; blend thoroughly. Sprinkle roast with salt and pepper and fill with bread crumb mixture. Stand on a rack in a roasting pan. Nick sides of bacon strips and place over stuffing. Place pieces of potato on tips of ribs to keep them from charring. Place in oven and roast about 30 minutes per pound. Place roast on platter. Remove bacon and potato. Keep warm while preparing gravy. Thicken pan drippings with a little flour; season to taste with currant jelly. Place paper frills on ribs and serve with gravy. Yield: 8 servings of two ribs each.

PARTY MEAT ROLLS

2 one-pound boneless steaks (chuck, round, rump or flank) , 1/2-inch thick
1/2 pound lean pork, ground
1/2 pound beef, ground
1/2 pound veal, ground
1 cup onion, chopped
2 cloves garlic, minced
1 1/2 teaspoons salt
1/2 teaspoon pepper
1/2 teaspoon thyme
1/2 teaspoon basil
1/2 teaspoon sweet marjoram
1 cup water
Flour

Trim steaks, removing fat and membrane. Place on a board and pound until thin, using edge of plate or mallet. Arrange ground meats in layers over steak, sprinkling each one with onion, garlic, salt, pepper and herbs. Roll the steaks, overlapping the edges, press into shape and wrap in cheesecloth. Tie firmly and place on rack roasting pan. Add the water. Bake in 350° oven until tender. Remove the meat rolls, unwrap, place on platter and keep warm while making the sauce. Blend 2 tablespoons flour with a little cold water, then stir into 1 cup of hot liquid. Bring to a boil and cook, stirring, till mixture is smooth and thick. Yields about 12 servings.

LIVER-AND-BACON ON SKEWERS

5 small tomatoes
1½ pounds calf liver, thickly sliced; or
     1½ pounds chicken livers
6 bacon slices
Seasoned salt
Pepper
1½ cups rice
1 beef-bouillon cube
3 tablespoons butter

Cut each tomato into 6 chunks. Cut calf liver into 36 pieces (leave chicken livers whole). Cut each bacon slice into 4 pieces. Arrange liver and tomato chunks and bacon pieces on each of 6 long skewers. Sprinkle with seasoned salt, pepper. Lay skewers across shallow baking pan, so they rest on edges of pan. Bake 20 to 25 minutes. Cook rice as label directs, first dissolving bouillon cube in the boiling water.

Serve liver-and-bacon on skewers with cooked rice, which has been tossed with butter. Serves 6.

I drove my Reindeer to the market,
And friendly neighbors helped me park it!

ROAST PHEASANT

Only young pheasant is desirable for broiling
or roasting. Clean and truss bird; salt inside;
stuff with Apple, Prune, or Bread Stuffing.
Roast in open roaster in moderate oven (350°)
until tender.

ROAST SQUAB

Clean squab. Rub inside with salt and pepper.
Brown giblets and add to ½ recipe Bread Stuffing; stuff squab; rub with butter; bake uncovered in moderate oven (350°) until tender,
about 45 to 60 minutes.

STANDING RIB ROAST

Standing rib roast
Salt
Pepper

Select a 2- or 3-rib standing roast (4 to 5 pounds). Place fat side up in roasting pan; season with salt and pepper and place in moderate oven (350°). Do not cover and do not add water. Allow 18 to 20 minutes per pound for rare roast, 22 to 25 minutes per pound for medium, and 27 to 30 minutes per pound for well-done roasts.

BAKED CHICKEN, FLORENCE

2 Broilers, 3 lbs. each, cut as for frying
Flour
2 eggs, beaten
Bread Crumbs
1/2 lb. butter
Salt
Pepper
Paprika

Season flour with salt, pepper, and paprika to taste. Dip pieces of chicken in seasoned flour, then in beaten eggs, and lastly in bread crumbs. Melt butter in baking dish, lay pieces of chicken in melted butter, and bake for 2 hours at 350°, turning chicken once so that both sides are properly browned, and increasing heat to 500° 10 minutes before serving to make chicken crisp. Serves 6.

STUFFED CABBAGE

2 pounds ground beef
1 large fresh cabbage
1 cup cooked rice
1 large minced onion
Sage, salt, pepper
2 small cans tomato paste
1 can tomatoes
3 Tbs. vinegar
2 Tbs. brown sugar
15 bay leaves
3 ginger snaps

Boil cabbage, head down, in covering water. Cook for a few minutes until slightly tender. Separate leaves. Mix together steak, rice, chopped onion, sage, salt, pepper, and about 3 teaspoons paste. Fill each cabbage leaf with a generous helping of the meat mixture, fold like an envelope, and lay in a large roasting pan. When cabbage leaves and meat have been used up, cover mixture with tomatoes, paste, 1 paste can of water, vinegar, brown sugar, bay leaves and ginger snaps. Cook covered for 3-4 hours. Serves 8.

POT ROAST CURRY

3 tablespoons shortening
1 medium onion, chopped
2 tablespoons celery, chopped
2 tablespoons green pepper, chopped
3 tablespoons flour
1½ tablespoons curry powder
Salt and pepper
1 can beef bouillon, undiluted
2 cups cooked pot roast, cubed
2 cups white rice, cooked

Sauté onion, celery, and green pepper 15 min-

Party Casseroles

CREOLE JAMBALAYA

2 tablespoons butter
1/2 cup chopped onion
1 clove garlic, crushed
1/4 pound cooked ham, diced (3/4 cup)
1 can (1 lb.) tomatoes, undrained
3/4 cup canned condensed chicken broth
1-1/2 pounds raw shrimp, shelled and deveined
1 tablespoon parsley, chopped
1 bay leaf
1 teaspoon salt
1/4 teaspoon dried thyme leaves
1/2 teaspoon Tabasco
1/8 teaspoon pepper
1 cup raw long-grain white rice

Preheat oven to 350°. In hot butter in Dutch oven, saute onion until soft — about 5 minutes. Add garlic and ham; saute 5 minutes longer. Stir in tomatoes, chicken broth, shrimp, parsley, bay leaf, salt, thyme, Tabasco, and pepper. Bring to a boil, covered. Pour into a 2-quart casserole. Sprinkle rice over top of mixture; gently press into liquid just until rice is covered. Do not stir. Cover. Bake 40 minutes, or until rice is tender and liquid is absorbed. Toss gently before serving. With a mixed green salad, this makes an excellent meal. Serves 6.

GOURMET TURKEY CASSEROLE

8 tablespoons butter
1½ cups celery, sliced
1 medium onion, minced
8 tablespoons flour
Salt and pepper
3½ cups milk
1 can condensed cream-of-mushroom
   soup, undiluted
2 cups cooked ham, cubed
2½ cups roast turkey, cubed
2 tablespoons pimiento, minced
¼ teaspoon dried basil
3 tablespoons cooking sherry
½ cup sharp American cheese, grated
Parsley sprigs

Sauté celery and onion in butter until just tender. Stir in flour, salt, pepper; add milk. Cook, stirring constantly, till sauce is thickened. Add soup, ham, turkey, pimiento, basil, sherry. Taste; add more seasonings if needed. Turn into 2-quart casserole; top with cheese and bake, uncovered, at 350°, 1 hour. Garnish with parsley. Makes 8 servings.

OYSTER CASSEROLE

1 cup fresh mushrooms, sliced
8 tablespoons butter
1 cup fine crumbs
2 pints oysters
1 cup milk
1/2 cup light cream

Saute sliced mushrooms in 2 tablespoons butter

for 2 minutes. Line bottom of greased casserole with 1/3 of crumbs, add a layer of sliced mushrooms and dot with 1 tablespoon butter; add another layer of crumbs, then oysters, remaining sliced mushrooms and a final layer of crumbs. Pour milk, cream and remaining 5 tablespoons butter, melted, over top. Bake in 350° oven 25 minutes. Serves 6.

FILLET OF SOLE LAURENT

8 tablespoons butter
2 tablespoons onion, chopped
3/4 teaspoon salt
1/8 teaspoon pepper
1 cup white wine
3 pounds sole or flounder fillets
4 tablespoons flour
1 cup milk
1 4-ounce can mushrooms

Melt 4 tablespoons of butter in frying pan, add onion, salt, pepper, and 1/3 cup of the wine. Cook fillets, a few at a time, slowly till they turn white (2 to 3 minutes); gently lift fish to shallow 3-quart casserole. Repeat until all are cooked; pour over it liquid remaining in skillet. Melt 4 remaining tablespoons butter over low heat; add flour, stir until blended and bubbly; remove from heat. Gradually stir in milk and remaining 2/3 cup wine; cook, stirring constantly, until slightly thickened. Pour over fish; top with mushrooms. Cover; bake in moderate oven (350°) for 20 minutes. Garnish with parsley. Makes 8 servings.

Let's pour some Yule-tide spirit
In a great big mixing bowl;
Then add a few ingredients,
And lo! a Casserole!

FISH SOUFFLÉ

4 tablespoons flour
¼ teaspoon salt
Dash pepper
½ cup mayonnaise
4 tablespoons milk
1 to 1¼ cups fish
2 tablespoons parsley, chopped
¼ teaspoon onion, grated
1 teaspoon lemon juice
4 egg whites

Mix mayonnaise, flour, salt and pepper. Add milk slowly. Stir in fish, parsley, onion, lemon

37

juice. Beat egg whites until stiff. Gently fold in mayonnaise mixture until thoroughly blended. Pour into a greased 7-inch casserole and bake in a slow oven (325°) 40 to 45 minutes. Serve at once. Yield: 4 servings.

Canned or cooked fresh fish may be used. Or use finely chopped cooked meats, minced chicken or vegetables. Or grated cheese, omitting parsley, onion and lemon juice.

TUNA POT PIE

1½ cups carrots, diced
1½ cups potatoes, diced
1 cup peas
3 tablespoons chopped onion
Milk
¼ cup butter
¼ cup flour
1 can tuna, chunk-style
½ teaspoon salt
¼ teaspoon pepper
1 cup pie crust mix

Cook vegetables until tender. Drain liquid, add enough milk to make 1¾ cups. Melt butter, blend in flour, add liquid. Stir until thickened. Pour over vegetables, add tuna and seasoning. Turn into greased 1½-quart casserole. Prepare pie crust mix according to package directions. Cover hot filling with pie crust, slash to release steam. Bake in a 400° oven for 25-30 minutes, or until crust is an appetizing brown. Serves 4 generously for luncheon or dinner.

SUCCOTASH CASSEROLE

1 large onion, chopped
2 tablespoons fat
2 cans cooked dried limas
1 cup chili sauce
6 whole cloves
2 cans whole-kernel corn, drained
1 teaspoon salt
Dash pepper
8 slices ham, turkey or capon

Sauté onion in fat over low heat in small frying pan 5 minutes, or just until tender. Mix undrained limas, drained corn, chili sauce, cloves, salt, pepper, and sautéed onion in large baking dish. Arrange meat slices on top of mixture in baking dish. Bake in moderate oven (350°) 45 minutes, or until bubbly hot. Serves 8.

CRAB AND OLIVE BAKE

1 cup ripe olives
2 eggs, hard-boiled
1 (6½ or 7-oz.) can crab meat
1 teaspoon onion, grated
1 teaspoon prepared mustard
¼ cup milk
½ teaspoon Worcestershire sauce
1 (10½-oz.) can cream-of-mushroom
   soup
¼ cup pimiento, diced
Buttered dry bread crumbs

Cut olives into large pieces. Dice eggs. Drain crab meat. Stir onion, mustard, milk and Worcestershire into soup. Blend in pimiento, olives, eggs and crab. Spoon into baking shells or shallow baking dish and top with crumbs. Bake in moderate oven (350°) 20 to 25 minutes, until thoroughly heated and browned on top. Makes 4 to 6 servings.

SAUERKRAUT, FRANKFURTER AND POTATO CASSEROLE

1 No. 2½ can sauerkraut
1 cup onion, finely chopped
2 tablespoons dark brown sugar
4 to 8 frankfurters
4 potatoes, medium-size
1 tablespoon butter, melted
Salt
Paprika

Turn sauerkraut, without draining it, into a baking dish (about 11 by 7 by 2 inches). Toss with onion and brown sugar. Bury frankfurters in the kraut. Peel potatoes and cut in half lengthwise; arrange on top. Brush with butter and sprinkle with salt and paprika. Bake in hot oven (425°) uncovered, for 30 minutes, or just until some of the top ends of the kraut brown a bit; cover tightly, and bake until potatoes are cooked through — 20 to 30 minutes longer. Serve at once from baking dish. Makes 4 servings — 1 to 2 frankfurters for each portion, depending on how many were used.

VEGETABLES
& SALADS

Vegetables & Salads

PERSILLADE POTATOES

12 to 18 new potatoes
1/4 cup butter, melted
1 tablespoon lemon juice
1/3 cup parsley, minced

Cook new potatoes in jackets; remove jackets when potatoes are done. Combine butter, lemon juice, and parsley; add potatoes; toss until coated. Serves 6.

POTATO PUFFS

2 cups cold mashed potatoes
2 tablespoons flour
Salt and pepper
1 egg
1 teaspoon baking powder

Blend well together in mixer. Drop a teaspoonful at a time in hot fat. Let fry slowly until the puffs become brown. When well puffed, place on brown paper to drain.

GLAZED ONIONS

18 small white onions
1 tablespoon butter
2 tablespoons sugar

Wash and peel onions; cover with water and cook until tender; drain. Melt butter and sugar; add onions and cook over low heat until golden brown, turning occasionally. Serves 6.

BAKED EGGPLANT
IN THE SHELL

1 eggplant
2 tablespoons butter
1 small onion, grated
¼ cup bread crumbs
1 egg yolk
¼ pound American cheese, grated

Parboil eggplant until tender, but not soft. Cut in half, crosswise. Scrape out the inside and mash with the butter, onion, bread crumbs, egg, cheese and salt and pepper to taste. Refill shells, place in pan in oven. Baste with butter and brown in 350° oven for approximately 40-50 minutes.

MINT-GLAZED CARROTS
WITH PEAS

3 medium-sized carrots, cut in strips
2 cups fresh peas
4 tablespoons butter
Salt and pepper
4 tablespoons sugar
¼ cup butter
½ tablespoon chopped mint leaves

Cook carrots in boiling, salted water 15 minutes; drain. Cook peas in boiling, salted water, about 8 to 10 minutes; drain and season with 2 tablespoons butter, salt, and pepper. Glaze carrot strips in mixture of sugar, 2 tablespoons butter, and mint leaves. Place peas in serving dish; add carrots.

CURRIED VEGETABLES

4 cups diced potatoes
1 package frozen cauliflower
2 packages mixed vegetables
12 white onions
¼ pound butter
½ teaspoon curry powder
¼ teaspoon salt
2 tomatoes
1 cup hot water

Parboil diced potatoes in salted water until nearly done. Put them in a heavy skillet with the 2 packages of frozen mixed vegetables, 1 package frozen cauliflower, 12 chopped white onions, ¼ pound butter, ½ teaspoon of curry powder, a little salt, 2 tomatoes, peeled and quartered and seeded, and a cup of hot water. Cover and simmer very gently, stirring occasionally, until vegetables are tender.

SQUASH AU GRATIN

5 small squash
4 tablespoons butter
Salt and pepper
2 eggs
Bread crumbs
¼ pound American cheese

Cut and boil squash. Drain and put through colander. Add butter and season. Add well beaten egg. Pour into buttered baking dish, cover with bread crumbs and grated cheese. Bake in moderate oven about 30 minutes.

Trim the tree with shouts of glee;
with laughter, song, and jollity!

GREEN BEANS WITH MUSTARD SAUCE

½ teaspoon dry mustard
½ teaspoon flour
¼ teaspoon salt
2 beaten egg yolks
¾ cup milk, scalded
2 tablespoons vinegar
4 cups hot green beans

Mix mustard, flour, and salt in double boiler; add egg yolks; beat well. Slowly add hot milk; cook until thick; add lemon juice. Pour over green beans. Serves 8. For best flavor, cut stem end of beans, and steam whole in very little water.

CARAWAY CABBAGE

6 onions	1 tablespoon vinegar
1 tablespoon butter	3 tablespoons sugar
½ cup water	1 cabbage
1 teaspoon caraway seed	

Shred cabbage, eliminating heart and hard part. Brown thinly sliced onions in melted butter, and set aside. Place cabbage and caraway seeds in ½ cup water and boil for about 30 minutes. Add onions, vinegar and sugar, and cook for another 10 minutes.

MUSHROOMS AND SOUR CREAM

1 pound mushrooms
3 tablespoons butter
1 cup sour cream
Salt and pepper to taste

Wash mushrooms. Place butter in skillet and sauté mushrooms. When tender add sour cream. Cook slowly until sauce is thickened. Season.

CAULIFLOWER WITH ALMONDS

1 head cauliflower
½ cup salted almond meats
2 cups white sauce

Trim leaves from stalk, leaving 1 inch of stem. Steam, tightly covered, using enough water to cover stem but not touching head. Cook about 25 minutes. To serve, cut off stalk and place cauliflower in serving dish. Stick almonds into cauliflower and pour white sauce over it.

TOMATO SALAD RING MOLD

1 can tomato soup
1 cup boiling water
1 tablespoon vinegar
Pinch of salt
1 onion, grated
1 package lemon jello
1 small clove of garlic, grated
4 stalks celery, diced
1 small jar stuffed green olives

Pour cup of boiling water over lemon jello and when it is dissolved add the can of tomato soup, salt and vinegar, stirring all until smooth. Then grate in the onion and garlic, holding grater over the bowl and allowing the juice to run into the mixture as well as the finely grated garlic and onion. Finally add chopped celery. Slice green stuffed olives and place them in the bottom of ring molds; fill these with mixture and chill in refrigerator.

Serve with lettuce leaves, and fresh cucumber.

PINEAPPLE AND CARROT MOLD

2 packages lemon jello
2 cups hot water
1 cup pineapple juice
1 cup cold water
1 cup crushed pineapple
1 cup carrots, grated

Make jello, add pineapple and carrots, and set in refrigerator to jell. Serve with mayonnaise thinned out with cream.

47

ANCHOVY SALAD BOWL

½ head lettuce
½ bunch escarole
1 bunch watercress
¾ cup Swiss cheese, cut in strips
2 ounces anchovy fillets

Break lettuce in small pieces in salad bowl. Tear escarole and watercress in small pieces and add to lettuce. Arrange Swiss cheese and anchovies over top. Pour over ¼ cup French dressing; toss lightly. Serves 6.

GARLIC CROUTONS FOR SALAD

Melt 2 tablespoons butter in medium-size frying pan; stir in ¼ teaspoon garlic powder. Dice 4 slices bread or leftover toast. Sauté slowly, stirring often, in melted butter mixture until cubes are well toasted on all sides. Store in a screwtop jar. Delicious tossed with a green salad or floated on top of soup.

CAVIAR SALAD DRESSING

½ cup mayonnaise
1 tablespoon horseradish
Squeeze of lemon juice
Small jar black caviar

Stir horseradish into mayonnaise. Mix well. Add lemon juice. Then fold in black caviar. Serve on hearts of lettuce. This quantity serves 4 persons.

FRENCH DRESSING

2 teaspoons sugar
½ teaspoon salt
½ teaspoon dry mustard
½ teaspoon paprika
¼ teaspoon black pepper
2 tablespoons lemon juice
¼ cup vinegar
¾ cup salad oil

Put ingredients in jar; and shake well.

THOUSAND ISLAND DRESSING

2 tablespoons chili sauce
1 cup mayonnaise
½ teaspoon Worcestershire sauce
1 teaspoon chopped olives
1 teaspoon chopped pimientos

Mix together and shake well before serving.

ROQUEFORT DRESSING

½ cup Roquefort cheese
1 cup French dressing
1 tablespoon fresh lemon juice
½ cup mayonnaise
1 clove garlic, pressed in garlic press
1 teaspoon dry mustard
1 tablespoon Worcestershire sauce

Beat cheese in bowl, with mayonnaise and
French dressing. Add other ingredients. Mix
well. Let stand 12 hours or longer. Add a bit of
crumbled Roquefort cheese before serving.

RUSSIAN DRESSING

¼ cup sugar
½ cup water
2 tablespoons chili sauce
½ teaspoon salt
1 tablespoon green pepper,
  finely chopped
Juice of 1 lemon
1 tablespoon vinegar
¼ cup catsup
1 tablespoon Worcestershire sauce
1 cup salad oil
¼ cup grated onion

Cook sugar and water until mixture spins a thread. Cool. Combine remaining ingredients; add syrup and shake thoroughly. Chill.

MUSTARD CREAM DRESSING

1 teaspoon dry mustard
½ teaspoon salt
2 teaspoons flour
3 teaspoons sugar
Cayenne pepper
2 egg yolks, beaten
⅓ cup vinegar
⅔ cup whipping cream

Combine mustard, salt, flour, sugar, cayenne pepper and add to egg yolks. Add vinegar slowly. Cook over boiling water, stirring constantly until thick. Cool. Whip cream until stiff and fold in.

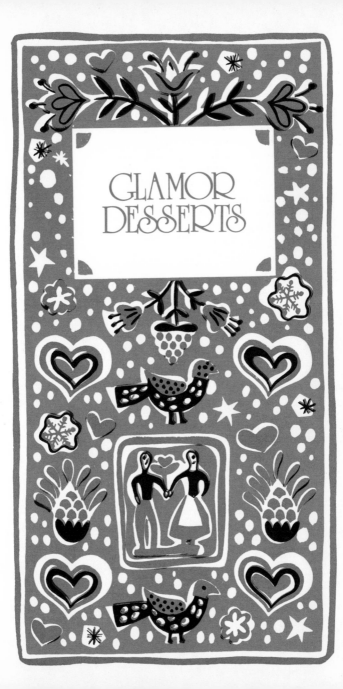

GLAMOR
DESSERTS

Glamor Desserts

PINEAPPLE TORTE

1 cup sifted cake flour
1 teaspoon baking powder
½ cup butter
1½ cups sugar
4 eggs, separated
5 tablespoons milk
1 teaspoon vanilla extract
1 No. 2 can crushed pineapple
1 cup heavy cream, whipped

Set oven at 350°. Sift together flour and baking powder. Cream butter until soft. Gradually add ½ cup sugar; continue creaming till fluffy. Mix in egg yolks. Add dry ingredients alternately with milk, mixing well after each addition. Spread dough evenly into 2 9-inch layer pans with removable bottoms or lined with paper or aluminum foil and greased. Beat egg whites until they hold soft peaks. Stir in vanilla. Gradually add remaining cup sugar and continue beating until meringue holds stiff peaks. Spread over dough. Bake 45 minutes. Cool 10 minutes, then carefully remove from pans and cool thoroughly. Drain pineapple, pressing out excess liquid, then mix with whipped cream. Place one of the torte layers, meringue side down, on a serving plate. Spread with whipped cream; top with second layer, meringue up. Decorate with candied cherries and pineapple. Chill at least 1 hour. Serves 10.

YEAST CAKE

½ pound butter
2 tablespoons sugar
Pinch of salt
3 egg yolks
1 envelope yeast, dissolved in
    ¼ cup water
2½ cups sifted flour
3 egg whites
1 cup sugar
1 cup broken walnut meats
½ cup raisins
Cinnamon

Cream the butter, add sugar and a pinch of salt. Separate eggs, and add the yolks which have been beaten until light in color. Then add the yeast which has been dissolved in luke-warm water, ¼ cup milk, and the sifted flour. Roll the dough into a ball and wrap well in wax paper. Place in refrigerator for 8 to 10 hours, or overnight.

Next Day. Beat the egg whites until stiff, folding in 1 cup sugar when eggs are beaten. Remove dough from refrigerator and separate into four parts, rolling each part into a rectangle about 8 x 16 inches. Spread egg whites onto the dough, and sprinkle with walnuts, raisins and cinnamon. Roll as for a jelly roll, and place the four rolls on a baking sheet, cut side down. Allow to rise for 1 hour in a warm place. Bake in a 325° oven for 25 minutes, or until done. Cool, and sprinkle with confectioners' sugar.

CONTINENTAL APPLE CAKE

Batter

2 cups flour
1 cup butter
2 egg yolks
2 tablespoons sugar
Juice and rind of 1 lemon
Bread crumbs

Mix flour, butter, egg yolks and sugar. Knead with hands. Add lemon juice and grated rind. When well blended and smooth, chill for several hours. Roll 1/4-inch thick. Divide in two parts and line an oblong tin with half the dough. Sprinkle with bread crumbs.

Fill with the following:

Filling

4 apples, thinly sliced
1/2 cup sugar
1/4 cup raisins
1 teaspoon cinnamon
1 egg white
Powdered sugar

Fill with sliced apples, sugar, raisins. Sprinkle with cinnamon. Cover with remaining dough. Brush top with slightly beaten egg white and bake in a 350° oven for 30 to 35 minutes or until apples are tender. Dust with powdered sugar and cut in squares. Serve hot or cold with whipped cream. Serves 6.

Let's have a glamorous dessert,
with cream and marshmallows!
We'll decorate the center with
Old Santa's cherry nose!

PEACH MERINGUE
AND RASPBERRIES

Thaw 2 packages frozen raspberries; put into
serving dish. Drain syrup from 8 peach halves.
Meanwhile beat 3 egg whites until stiff but not
dry. Gradually beat in 6 tablespoons sugar; beat
till smooth and glossy. Place peaches, cut side
up, in shallow baking dish; top each with
meringue; bake in 450° oven for 4 to 5 minutes.
Remove peaches carefully and float on raspberries.

DEVIL'S FOOD CAKE

2 cups sifted cake flour
1 teaspoon soda
1/4 teaspoon salt
1/2 cup butter or shortening
1 1/4 cups sugar
3 egg yolks, beaten till very thick and
    lemon colored
3 ounces unsweetened chocolate, melted
1 cup milk
1 teaspoon vanilla

Set oven at 350°. Grease 2 9-inch layer-cake pans.
Sift flour, soda and salt together twice. Cream
butter, until soft and smooth. Gradually add
sugar and continue creaming until mixture is
light and fluffy. Add egg yolks and beat thoroughly, then beat in melted chocolate. Add 1/4
of the flour mixture and stir just until blended.
Gently blend in 1/3 of the milk. Repeat until all
flour and liquid are used. Stir in vanilla. Pour
into pans and bake 25 minutes or until cake
tester inserted in center comes out clean and
dry. Let cool in pans 5 minutes, then turn out
and finish cooling the layers before spreading
with frosting.

Chocolate Frosting

3 ounces chocolate, unsweetened
4 tablespoons butter
1 1/2 cups sifted confectioners' sugar
1/4 cup milk
1 egg

Melt chocolate in double boiler. Remove from heat, add butter and stir till well blended. Add remaining ingredients and beat till mixture is fluffy and of good spreading consistency. Spread between cooled devil's food layers, and over top and sides. Serves 10-12.

RASPBERRY CREAM PIE

2 cups milk
1 teaspoon vanilla
½ cup sugar
⅓ cup flour
¼ teaspoon salt
4 egg yolks
1 whole egg
¼ cup heavy cream, whipped
1 baked 9-inch pie shell
1 pint raspberries
1 cup red currant jelly

Scald milk with the vanilla in a double boiler. Combine sugar, flour and salt. Blend in a little of the scalded milk, then stir mixture into remaining milk. Cook in top of double boiler till thick, stirring often. Beat together the egg yolks and whole egg. Gradually stir in milk mixture. Return to double boiler and cook over simmering water, stirring constantly, till thick enough to coat a metal spoon. Strain and cool. Fold whipped cream into cooled egg mixture. Turn into baked pie shell. Cover with raspberries. Melt jelly over low heat, stirring constantly, and pour or brush evenly over berries. Serves 8.

Weary hostess, shed no tear,
Christmas comes but once a year!

BANANA CREAM PIE

1 baked 9-inch pie shell
½ cup sugar
5 tablespoons flour
¼ teaspoon salt
2 cups milk
2 egg yolks, slightly beaten
1 tablespoon butter
½ teaspoon vanilla extract
3 ripe bananas
½ pint sweet cream, whipped

Combine sugar, flour and salt in top of double boiler. Gradually stir in milk. Cook over rapidly boiling water until well thickened, stirring constantly. Then cook 10 minutes longer, stirring occasionally. Blend a small amount of the hot milk mixture into the beaten egg yolks, then pour back into remaining milk mixture, stirring vigorously. Cook 1 minute longer. Remove from heat; stir in butter and vanilla. Cool. Peel and slice bananas; place slices in pie shell and cover immediately with cooled filling. Top with slightly sweetened whipped cream. Serves 8.

HOLIDAY PRUNE PIE

½ pastry recipe
2¾ cups cooked prunes, pitted
1 egg
⅓ cup granulated sugar
⅛ teaspoon salt
1 tablespoon lemon juice
½ cup liquid from prunes
½ cup brown sugar, packed
¼ cup flour
½ teaspoon cinnamon
3 tablespoons soft butter

Heat oven to 450°. Prepare unbaked 9-inch pie shell. Arrange prunes in shell. In small bowl, beat egg; blend in granulated sugar, salt, lemon juice, and prune liquid; pour over prunes. Blend brown sugar, flour, cinnamon, and butter until crumbly; sprinkle over prunes. Bake 10 minutes. Reduce heat to 350°; bake 20 to 30 minutes longer, or until set in center. Serves 6-8.

Apricots may be substituted for prunes, and the apricot liquid used instead of the prune liquid. Soak diced apricots overnight, stew lightly in water to cover, with a very little sugar.

SOUR CREAM APPLE PIE

3 pounds tart apples, pared, cored and sliced
¾ cup sugar
½ teaspoon cinnamon
Dash nutmeg
¼ teaspoon salt
½ cup sour cream

Set oven at 425°. Roll out half the pastry to desired thickness; line a 9-inch pie pan, trimming edges even with rim of pan. Spread half the apples over the pastry. Combine sugar, cinnamon, nutmeg and salt. Sprinkle half the mixture over the apples. Repeat layers of apples and sugar mixture; top with sour cream. Roll out remaining pastry and place over filling. Trim edges and seal. Slash top in several places to let steam escape. Bake 10 minutes at 425°, then lower heat to 375° and bake about 30 minutes longer or until apples are tender. Serves 8.

FRENCH APPLE TART

½ cup butter
1 tablespoon sugar
½ teaspoon salt
1 egg
2 cups sifted flour
¼ cup cold water
2 cups applesauce
3 cups apple slices
½ cup powdered sugar
½ cup apricot jam

Set oven at 375°. Cream butter with sugar and

salt until mixture is light and fluffy. Add egg
and beat well. Mix in flour, using fingers or a
pastry blender. Add enough water to make a
stiff dough; stir just to mix. Roll dough to $\frac{1}{4}$-
inch thickness; place in 9-inch spring-form pan.
Press dough over bottom of pan and up around
sides to height of 1 inch. Prick bottom of pastry
with fork and spread with apple sauce. Arrange
apple slices over apple sauce, overlapping the
slices and making a spiral design. Sprinkle with
powdered sugar and bake about 40 minutes or
until apples are tender and crust is brown. Heat
apricot jam till thin and smooth. Pour or brush
evenly over apples. Serve the tart either warm
or cold. Serves 8.

QUICK SOUTHERN PECAN PIE

1 cup sugar
$\frac{1}{4}$ cup melted butter
$\frac{1}{2}$ cup corn syrup
3 well-beaten eggs
1 cup pecans
1 unbaked pie shell

Mix sugar, syrup and butter; add eggs and pecans. Fill unbaked pie shell with mixture and
bake for 10 minutes at 400° then for 30 to 35
minutes at 350°. Serve either cold or hot. Delicious topped with slightly sweetened whipped
cream.

To decorate pie, use halved pecans as a border
on the whipped cream, which can be squeezed
through a pastry tube to form rosettes.

63

MOUSSE AU CHOCOLAT

½ pound sweet chocolate
6 eggs
6 tablespoons powdered sugar
Lady fingers

If possible, use chocolate that does not contain cocoa butter and break it into small pieces in a bowl. Pour boiling water over the chocolate to cover, and then cover the bowl with a large plate. After 5 minutes, carefully pour off the water and stir the chocolate with a fork, gradually adding the sugar while doing so. Beat the egg yolks slightly and stir them into the chocolate. Beat the egg whites until stiff and fold them into the egg and chocolate mixture until thoroughly blended. Pour into a serving dish and refrigerate for at least 6 hours. Serve with lady fingers. Makes 6 portions.

The mousse may also be served in individual portions as follows: Use tall champagne or parfait type glasses. Pour a jigger of Crème de Cacao into each glass and then fill with mousse. Top with a candied violet or a whole marron glacé.